Living With Abusive Parents

An Autobiography of Jessica Bourquin

DORRANCE
PUBLISHING CO
EST. 1920
PITTSBURGH, PENNSYLVANIA 15238

Dorrance Publishing Co
585 Alpha Drive
Pittsburgh, PA 15238
Visit our website at *www.dorrancebookstore.com*

ISBN: 979-8-88729-421-6
eISBN: 979-8-88729-921-1

MOM

I don't care if no one believes me about this, but this is my life. I am writing it down now so that I can finally put it behind me or give to a therapist if I decide to ever go back. I am done trying to tell everyone what I went through and no one listening. Huge trigger warning, if something triggers you, most likely I have had it happen to me.

My first memory is what it is like to drown. The weight of water filling my lungs and needing to breath. Every fiber of my being just screaming at me to lift my head to oxygen and get air. I learned later in life that my brother was trying to drown me about six months old. Before I was two years old, my brother had tried drowning me, poisoning me, causing illness, starving me, as well as setting the house on fire. I only know the poisoning because I remember what bleach tastes like. My parents don't remember me being anywhere near the chemicals as they were in tall cabinets. I know I was starved because as my father told me that as a kid I would have to go two or three days without an ounce of food because he wasn't home. When he got home, I would eat more than a grown man would, and then be OK. I will point out that my family, until I was two, was my mom, brother, sister, and dad. My dad worked two jobs, while my mom worked two jobs as well. My brother and sister are completely mental as well. How I survived until now and am able to be more sane than them is actually insane.

After I turned two years old, my mom and dad decided to divorce. Later I learned she left him because my mom heard he was messing with little girls in town. Now I believe it, but when she first told me, I didn't believe it. My brother was sent back to live with his dad after setting fire to the house, so he was out of my life until I was in middle school, mostly. My sister was sent to my grandma's as she was showing signs of being unstable. She threw me, trying to hit the wall but missing, because I wouldn't play with her. She also locked me in my room for over twelve hours because I refused to cook her food. Keep in mind, I am under two years old;

I can't cook! However, she said that she can't cook food; it's my job to. She was in and out of my life for years. You'll see her pop up here and there in my story.

Before we ended up in the car, I remember that my mom moved us into my aunt and uncle's house where they had their favorite child living with them. I don't have many memories about this time. However, I do remember that during this time I learned how to cut vegetables and what a hospital is. I wasn't allowed to eat any veggies unless it was cut to small manageable pieces and knowing that I asked my cousin if he would cut it. However he said, "Your what? Three? Learn how to cut them yourself, and don't bother me." So I learned how to use a knife and other utensils after that. I also remember after my cousin spent over an hour in the bathroom, not even showering, he left the bathroom and I went in, slipped and split my lip open on the toilet seat. Instead of sending me to the ER my aunt packed me in the car, drove me to my mom's job and left me there. Mom had to take me to the ER to fix my lip after her manager saw a kid standing at the door of their closed shop. The next morning she took me to a guy's house, told me to sit outside on the steps and stay there until she is done. I sat next to a red ant hill unfortunately. She saw me swollen and dragged me home after her visit, packing her bags right away, and we moved into the car.

After the divorce, my mom went back to college for music therapy. We were living homeless, inside of a car until I was three-and-a-half years old. This is the time I learned what sex is as she slept with her professors in the car. I only remember two of these people being there, but I remember it. She also taught me how to steal food from stores back then. My last memory of that car, however, is when the towing company brought a huge trash can to toss the broken car in it. It wasn't even a car at that point; it was twisted metal. My mom has no memory of most of my early childhood, including being in the car with me. I also remember being in the car but not in the accident. I don't know what happened, but I know something did.

At three-and-a-half, my mom sent me to my grandma's house. Now most of the time that would be amazing, however, it wasn't for me. My sister was still there in the house, and my grandmother was worse. Every morning I was not allowed to eat my food until my grandmother, grandfather, and sister were done. My food was cold by then as they had placed it before I was allowed to eat. I remember after the other two left, my grandma let me come into the dining room and eat my food while she watched. It was always cold oatmeal, with frozen raspberries on it. If I didn't finish it in five minutes, she would then stand up and force my head until it was inches from my food and told me to finish it now. I had to have it done on her time. If I cried in pain, she would slap me hard. After breakfast I was dragged outside and not allowed inside at all until it was starting to grow dark. I should point out, I have a unique sun allergy that makes it hard for me to be in the sun. She didn't care. I had to stay outside all day.

Grandfather would come out after an hour, and work on his garden. He didn't ever talk to me while out there, and would try to ignore me. He did leave me some of the garden's harvest when he went inside, so I had something to munch while outside. My sister told me he used to go out and get some McDonald's sometimes and would sneak it in to my sister's room. No one could do that for me, however, because of my "room." When I went to my grandma's, she had three bedrooms, and one bathroom. The master was theirs, the old child's room was my sister's, and the guest room was empty. I was forced to sleep on the couch in the living room every day instead of a bed. Grandma would say it's because I would get the guest bed dirty and she didn't want to do the laundry from in there. I also remember that she hated my curly hair and would use that horrible smelly hair gel that makes your hair turn into a helmet. She would use at least half the bottle every day we were leaving the house. Which does include Sunday as my family has been deeply Christian. The only good memory I have is when we went to an amusement park, as my granddad said he wanted to see his grandkids playing at a theme park. My sister actually put me on top of a tall slide and left me there knowing I was deeply afraid of heights. I don't remember who saved me. However, I remember curling in a ball and just sitting there for hours. I already had stopped crying at anything by this time in my life. Crying did nothing but bring pain to me.

When I was about to start kindergarten, my new stepdad heard my mom had a child and demanded I move in with them. So I moved to live with them in another state. He was a pastor in a church in this town, and so thankfully the town were nice to me. When I started talking to my mom, she noticed I couldn't say R. I was immediately put into speech therapy and as soon as I got home, Mom told me I am not allowed to talk in the house until I could say R correctly. It took until

I was in second grade before I could say R. Every time I tried to say anything I would be locked in the mud room of the church for six hours without anything but my clothes. I remember walking to and from school on my own every day as well from the church as my mom refused to walk me over. My stepdad didn't care enough, and so I was always alone to school.

When one of the breaks started, my stepbrother came to live with us during the break. My stepbrother asked his dad what sex was, and that is when my world crashed down. My stepfather came into my room and stripped me down. He pointed out what the female parts were using me, and then proceeded to hold me down on the bed while directing his son on how to fuck a girl. My first time was with my own stepbrother, and my screams were never heard. When I told my mom what happened, instead of helping me, she said it was my fault. She told me if I hadn't spread my legs for him it wouldn't happen. She then proceeded to take all the food from the house, and refused to feed me for a month. Thankfully school lunches were free for the pastor's kid. And my speech therapist would give me lunches during weekends. While I should have spoken up, my stepdad was the pastor. My little kid's brain told me no one would believe they would do anything to me as he is a man of god. My stepbrother did come into my room every night for the month he was with us. Once he left, my mom put food back into the house, but still refused to let me eat with the family.

As with most abusers, they will give you something to make you feel good. My stepdad got me a cat. I named her Pretty Kitty and she taught me how to survive in this world. She broke my violin after my mom forced me to take lessons. She wanted me to be super musically inclined like she was. Besides the speech therapy twice a week, I took piano lessons twice a week and then violin lessons once a week. Each lesson I was driven to, but I was expected to walk home, except the speech one as my mom didn't want to waste money on me having that. Kindergarten is also the first and last time my mom went to a parent-teacher conference about me. I remember being proud that my teacher was telling my mom I figured out how to make skin color with just the basic colors given the little kids. She told my mom that I have an eye for colors and would do well as an artist. While she did agree with her, when I got home all my art supplies were taken from me, and thrown into the fire. She also locked me in my room the entire weekend. This is also the year that when I woke up on Christmas Eve to see my mom wrapping presents was when she told me Santa didn't exist. That was my last Christmas she ever celebrated with me. I also remember her taking all my gifts from me and giving them to the kids who came to service that Christmas. So I ended up with no gifts that year sense Santa didn't exist and presents were for children who deserved them.

At first grade my stepdad lost his job, due to health reasons. So we moved to his home in another state and this is when my mom had to get a job to support us. The trip to and from the state, my mom and stepdad left me in a hotel room one night, and didn't come back for me for three days. Thankfully the hotel staff let me stay in the room and charged my mom for the extra days. We did bring Pretty Kitty with us though, and most of my good memories of her were in that house. She slept with me every night, refusing to leave me. I got a pixel light toy from my dad in this house, and I remember that I would put one light in and Pretty Kitty would attempt to put one in too. It was the worst picture ever but my chosen mom did it with me. I also remember getting a giant foam puzzle from him, and after building it, I told everyone to wipe their feet on it before entering my room. In the next few days I noticed claw marks—Pretty Kitty was cleaning her paws and claws before entering my room. This also when she got pregnant as my mom wouldn't let me or her in if the sun was out. I told her to have her kids in my plastic pink suitcase, using my favorite doll blankets to have her kids stay warm on. My mom was furious when she had placed about twenty spots for Pretty Kitty and she took my suitcase. I came home from school one day, and my mom was screaming. Pretty Kitty hid all her babies when my mom moved them to another bed, and threw my own suitcase away. She led me to each child and let me take them back to the new bed, but when my mom got close to a kitten, she clawed my mom so hard she bled. She was never violent before this day, but she was mad at my mom that day. Every day when I could go back inside, Pretty Kitty would teach me how to take care of her little ones. If she was feeding and one of them couldn't find a spot, she would look at me until I placed it in a good spot. She taught me what it is like to love and take care of something more than me. It still hurts remembering her, but I spent enough time on her.

Going back to how horrible my house was besides Pretty Kitty, my mom told me after moving here that I had to work for food. If I wanted to eat Sunday dinner,

I had to make at least $1 depending on how much work she put into the food. Chores didn't count, as chores are expected of children to do. This is also the house I remember that when I did dishes for the first time, I didn't clean one dish perfectly. When Mom saw that, she took all the dishes out of the cabinets, even ones that were clean and told me I had to wash them all. She also turned on the water to scalding hot, shoved my hands under the water and screamed that this is how hot the water must be to do dishes. If the water was lukewarm or even colder than this, she would have to redo all the dishes again. She came in every five minutes to see if my water was still that hot. Even now I still have issues doing any of the dishes in my own house.

After week of not having food, I realized I have to find some way to get food. I couldn't keep just asking my classmates for some of their lunches, as lunches were not free anymore. I went into the woods where the main church was and asked the pastor if there is anything I could do to gain some kind of money. He told me, if my mom or dad approve, I could work on his farm and bring some of the harvests home. He just assumed we were hard pressed for money, never that I was told to work. I worked in his fields twice a week and got to bring some food home, but that still didn't count for actual money. I learned I could gather cans from the house and areas around, and the pastor's wife would give me $0.05 for each can. She loved reusing them for small planters herself. I did start eating some of the harvest before I went home as after my first day, Mom took my food. She told me I am too spoiled to be allowed to eat food. Day two I ate some of the food before I got home, just to keep my energy up.

After a couple of months of doing this, I realized that Mom was forcing me to pay too much. I would take my money to the local grocery store four blocks away and buy small groceries that I knew how to cook, like mac and cheese. Easy things with small instructions and easy clean up. I don't remember Mom making a single meal for me after I started buying my own food, not even as an adult and I was forced back to her. My mom has never cooked for me except one day, the day after I called my dad to rescue me. But that wasn't until ninth grade. Thankfully though, my stepdad stopped messing sexually with me after moving to this house.

In second grade, Mom and I left my stepdad and Pretty Kitty several states away. Turns out he had brain cancer, which is why he was paranoid about everything. Mom didn't feel safe, so she dragged me away without my chosen mom. She promised we would go get her again but we never did. We moved to my aunt and uncle's house. This is when I learned how to pick locks as well as how to open windows, and leave no evidence of either. My mom wasn't really in my life at this time. I don't remember her in this house at all. I learned that my mom was in and out of the psychiatric ward the time we were there. So here is about my aunt and uncle's abuse, as it still goes on.

My aunt locked me in my room as soon as my mom went into the ward, saying I was unstable and not allowed out of my room until 8:00 p.m. She also told me I have to go to bed at 7:30 p.m. She brought me food every other day, but I wasn't allowed out, even for the bathroom. However, Sunday I was allowed out all day, as it is a holy day. I was allowed to play with my toys my dad had sent on that day as well. However, I was only allowed one hour max in the bathroom per month, and every time I needed the bathroom I had to leave the door open. I do remember going to school for that half of a year, but I don't remember my school life. I only remember being locked up as soon as I got home. I learned how to pick locks after my aunt and uncle decided to leave for a day. Best day ever in the house, being all alone.

After a month or so after moving there, Mom apparently got out of the ward and my aunt took me to go pick her up. However, after getting her, my aunt didn't pay attention to the gas, and ended up making us stranded in the middle of nowhere in the middle of the night. She said she would get gas as it was her fault, and left Mom and me in the car. This is when Mom told me she got a letter from my stepdad that he had cancer and that Pretty Kitty had died. As soon as I heard my chosen mom died, I sobbed for the first time in years.

Mom let it go for thirty seconds and then told me, "It's just a cat. Get over it." When I kept going, she slapped me and told me to grow up. If she hears me cry about her again she will leave me here and go home with my aunt alone. I stopped quickly, and have never cried in front of her again. She did end up taking me to and from her boytoys' houses when she needed me. This is where I started showing more signs of being carsick more. One day I told her I was going to throw up, and asked to pull over. She refused and after I started throwing up, she pulled over. I jumped out and kept going, that is until she came over and smacked me hard over my head. I have never been able to be sick since except when I was extremely sick with food poisoning many years later. She then threw paper towels at me and told me to clean the car. Once the car was clean she told me to walk back to town, and left me there. I did walk back to town, and by the time I got to the edge of town, she picked me back up and drove me home. During summer break we moved again to another state.

Now a lot of this one is mixed up and I will try to keep it decently straight as I was in this state for third grade to the last half of fourth grade. However, a lot more bad and good things happened here. When we moved down here. We lived in a townhouse while I was in Catholic school. The school only lasted for about a month before it got shut down due to a lice infestation. My mom moved us to my grandma's for about two weeks while Grandma used everything she could to get rid of the lice without removing all my hair. Including putting mayo on my head for four hours outside. When we went back to our townhouse, my brother and sister had been brought back after this so she could be a good mom to her kids. Well, my brother was addicted to weed, and my sister was already trying to get in everyone's pants. My brother is only ten years older than me, my sister four years older than me. I remember hiding in the closet my mom and I shared when my brother had a moment of clarity and tried to yell at my mom to give me up. He said while he may not be stable, he's more stable than she is. Him and his father would take care of me, if she would just sign the line. He tried so hard when his mind was clear to get me out of the house. It turns out he was autistic, so the weed helped him be clear but Mom refused to help his "addiction."

It was in this house that my brother and sister pushed me down the stairs of the townhouse. When my wrist got messed up, they dragged me out of the house, barefoot, to Mom's work five blocks away. We passed an ER to get to her work, just so they could tell her I fell down the stairs and I might need a doctor. She immediately sent us back to the ER, where I got a wrist brace as it was just sprained. My brother also came into our room one night with a clean pair of underwear on his head with a beer can in his hand. My sister and him had been drinking beer and he was drunk off his ass. Mom took a picture of it, and I remember most of this house thanks to that night. This is also the house that Mom and I shared a bedroom and she told me my breathing and heartbeat is loud. I needed to find a way to quiet it down or I would sleep outside in the cold. I still have to remind myself to breathe sometimes, as I can just forget to breathe thanks to spending time there. I do also remember learning how bad my brother was when for a full day, he told me my toes looked cute. He said this all day, even taking pictures of them. He never got actually diagnosed for his mental health, just a side note. He was Native American however, and after a small while, his dad reminded my mom he couldn't get any of the government money while he's in her care. So she sent him back after Christmas, and a month after our move.

My mom decided to take my sister and me to her boyfriend's house in the middle of nowhere. He was the most amazing man I have from my childhood. I have so many good memories from him, but I want to point out that my sister and I shared a room the whole time we were there. I remember being told by him the main reason that the bus came to me for school at all is because his parents and him sold parts of their land to make the city what it was. He used to own the whole area the town was in, so he was always included in everything there. He was already in his late sixties when we moved in with him. His farm was so wonderful and he taught me how to farm as well as how to live on my own. He taught me the importance of farm work, how to get livestock, and even how to hunt in the forest. While he could see my mom didn't care about me, he never spoke up. Instead he made sure I would survive no matter what happened to me. I remember that when we moved in, he had one dog, and ten cats. When we left, he had two chickens, thirteen cats, one dog, and four goats. He got me twelve chicken eggs for easter to raise. Wanted me to have something to take care of. Turns out it was ten chicken eggs and two duck eggs, but they were all dyed thanks to easter. I helped the runt and she was the most beautiful chicken ever when she grew up. Pure white with tiny blue spots everywhere, her dyed egg was blue just like her spots. Later on he got me three goats at an auction, one died due to age, but turned out one of them was pregnant. Ended up with four goats instead of three.

This place is also where I learned that I should never go to Mom with something serious. I was biking around the road one day and I fell off my bike, breaking my thumb. The puppy was with me, a beautiful golden retriever. After I fell he walked me home, as I couldn't bike anymore because of my tears and pain. I almost fell over twice, and he held me up each time, I wasn't that big still. When

I got home, Mom saw me, yelled at me for ripping up my clothes. I lay down on the loveseat, and when she saw my thumb she told me to stop being a drama queen and was about to move my thumb to point out it was fine when he came in from the forest. He saw my state and put me in the car. I remember hearing him yell at her because she wasn't taking care of me like she should. That puppy followed me everywhere when I had my cast on. He even helped me keep the food chest open while I dished out everyone's food daily. Farm life doesn't end just because you have a broken finger. I also remember a nail going through my hand here when I fell from the shed's step. Every time I got hurt he would take me to the hospital. However, my mom left him a few months after my cast came off, right about fourth grade, because my sister was claiming that he raped her. We were still in the same room; he never raped her. But she did what she wanted; we moved into another town in the same state.

Mom sent me to school, and this is when my sun allergy started getting back. I have a unique allergy, I used to sneeze uncontrolled in the sun. I couldn't stop until I was in the shade for thirty minutes. Even florescent lights would trigger it, just not as strong. Mom had no choice but to call my dad as she still refused to take me to the doctor. He told her he has the same issue, and with a pair of sunglasses, I should be able to control the sneezing more. I still had to wear them inside, and Mom got us blackout curtains to keep the sneezing to a minimum. She didn't want people to know her child wasn't perfect. This school I learned what chess is, and joined the chess club. I also learned I was good at logic puzzles as well. I just didn't have the drive to apply myself enough to pursue anything like that. When my chess club teacher suggested to my mom that maybe I should see if I have ADD or something else that would explain what is going on, she packed our bags and my sister and I moved with her back to my aunt and uncle's house. Moving there, I was sharing a room with two of my second cousins as well as my oldest cousin's wife. He moved out two days after I moved in, but I shared that room with them the whole time. My other cousin, the one who refused to cut my food as a child, shared the room his parents were in as well as my mom. Not much happened here, except that my sister wasn't in the house somehow, I don't know how.

Shortly after moving to that monstrosity of a house, and I mean it is still painted in three different colors per level, we moved to the attic of a family. My sister came back here for two weeks before she left. I learned later that my sister called social services while my mom was at work to tell them they got into a huge fight and she no longer feels safe. She was taken into foster care after that, and she was in and out of the house a lot through the rest of my life. This house, turns out Mom got asbestos poisoning from it. The ceiling above the bed that we slept in was unfinished and as such Mom learned recently that she got asbestosis from it. I don't know if I have it yet as no doctor will talk to me about health issues, but I will get to that later. This is the same place that I learned how to decorate cookies as well as cakes. Mom would buy blank cakes and cookies, teach me how to decorate them, and then not allow me to eat. I learned in this house that back then that social services couldn't take a kid out due to starvation if at least one loaf of bread was in the house. It didn't matter if the kid was not allowed to eat it, let alone look at it, there is bread, and as such, they are not starved. We lived there until somewhere in fifth grade. Mom and I moved into a trailer with my new stepdad at that time.

I learned what a computer was back then thanks to him, and at this point, Mom pointed out she only married him for the money. He was disabled thanks to work, and got a hefty chunk of money every month. She gained a gambling addiction at this point, while he was a gambler, he also only ever played Heroes of Might and Magic III. Here he had a dog, but because we were not allowed animals, that dog was left in the van. Because he had been living in the van for a long time, there were no back seats so the dog had enough space. It was horrible, and every time we left the house, we used the van. I remember I almost hit my head on the door one time, and at that point the dog became my seat belt. She would lay around me, putting her head and back legs around my lap. It helped out, but we only had her for a short time because the landlords told us to get rid of her. Thankfully we found a nice family that took her in, but she was so nice for that short time. We got rid of that van shortly after that happened and got a proper car.

In this house my mom was trying to hide that she was abusing me a lot more, as now both of her kids didn't want her and pointed that out to anyone who would listen. She didn't want to show that I was badly abused either. The first trailer I remember, my mom bought me a parakeet, which I named Dixie, and told me while she can't get me a cat this bird is my new pet. I loved Dixie his whole life, and I lived with him for a long time. The only real abuse she did to me in this house is I was on the top bunk of the bed when my sister came to visit, and I fell out, landing on my back on the floor. Instead of taking me to a doctor she just told me to go back to bed, and I installed the railings after finding them in her room. There wasn't much that happened in that trailer park, except that I wasn't allowed inside while the sun was out, and I wasn't allowed to eat in the house. If I wanted food, I would have to figure out how to get food outside instead of inside. She also had me taking thousands of health meds as well as meal supplements. I remember this green gook, that I was to drink daily. After a week of drinking it in front of her, I was allowed to take it to my room. I kept pouring it out of the window, this thing was chunky even after going through four strainers, and after a week the grass was dying out my window. I also remember that I was stealing my stepdad's soda as at this point I wasn't allowed water unless the green gunk was in it. Soda became my drink, Big Red to be perfectly honest. She did try to get my stepdad and I to start our own business, mind you I haven't even hit middle school when she started the business trip. We had to make money if we wanted to do anything. My friend and I hung outside a lot, and knowing that I needed to get groceries for my mom we tried to make a wagon out of scraps so I could get them more as I was biking to the store and school. The store was a twenty-five-minute bike from home, and school was almost one hour from home.

The last trailer we had in there, we got a cat who gave birth to five kittens. The mom, Midnight, was using Mom's bed as a litterbox, and as such when the kittens were old enough to survive without her, she took her to the country and dumped her. She then sold two of the kittens to someone else. So at this point, I had three kittens and a bird. Within the first month I had to find a home for the other kitten, and my friend was happy to have a black kitty. So I kept the two, Cookie and Tiger. This home is also where I learned that my stepdad didn't care who lived with him, his computer is more important than anything. I had twisted my ankle so bad one day from a bike ride that I couldn't walk without screaming. So I took his spare set of crutches to go to school, and when I got home, Mom ripped them from my arms grabbed me by the hair and threw me into my room. I wasn't allowed out of that room for anything for a week except to go to school. She told me I made her look bad because I went to school injured. At some point I started middle school, but I am not sure when, but I remember moving to the town over for Mom's business. The towns are so close together that it doesn't matter if we moved to either town, I would go to the same school system. Elementary was in the first town, middle and high school was in the town over. When we moved to the other town, was somewhere in sixth grade, though, as I remember getting on the bus in the trailer park for the other town, but I also remember my high school bully meeting me and my new house in sixth grade.

At this point, most of middle school was just school bullying, which most people are kind of used to. For me I just ignored her when she was mean, and friendly with her when she was nice. I figured I had enough going on at home that I can deal with her, and if she is mean to only me, then everyone else would have a better life in school. Besides I was used to being the new kid in schools and being bullied all the time for the sunglasses, my book love, my art, my parents, my clothes, everything. When we had moved to the first place in this town, Mom owned three businesses at once, in three buildings set up together. The first huge space she used for a mini-mall. The mini-mall had a spare room above it, that my aunt and uncle used when my aunt was running her business out of one of my mom's buildings.

The next business was much bigger, even though the building was super small. She ran her music therapy out of it, her wedding chapel, and my aunt's massage parlor. The wedding chapel stayed with her for years. Then the last one was our apartments above the wedding chapel, the mini-mall, and the empty building. There was five spare "bedrooms" besides the apartment that we lived in that had a computer room, two bedrooms, and a bathroom. So my mom rented out two of the spare rooms, gave another to my brother, another to my sister, and the last one was rented for a short time by an author. This is where a lot more trauma happened, we haven't hit the end at all. Even saying that this is almost the end of the chapter of my "childhood" trauma.

After school I was sent to the mini-mall to take over the selling of items as well and managing the store as while I was in school my aunt took care of it. After school I ran the whole thing until close, even closing up the shop, it was my main home. Mom couldn't control me there then because she was so busy in the other shop, that I was able to play games on the work computer, as well as use the bathroom there. After I closed to shop, I would have to tell my aunt its closing time, so she could go over there to lock up fully. I learned about my love of boots there as when we moved in, there was a shoe vendor there that let me chose whatever shoes I wanted. We never sold much in the mini-mall, probably due to location. However when my aunt and uncle left, things got bad. I started looking for ways to leave that house, I was in Yahoo chats offering sex to get out, since I didn't have any money thanks to Mom stealing my money for years. After my bully found out, she told my stepdad. After close one day, he came up to me, pulled me into my aunt and uncle's old room and raped me there. This kept going every day for three months. I never told my mom because of her reaction the first time. I just put up with it. However, the Yahoo messages stopped.

Now at this time I did get a paper route to get some legitimate money to pay for school lunches and dinners. I took two of them to make about $150 a month. One of them thanks to the length was $100 on its own. However, if you're a minor, your parents can pick up your check. After my first payment, I never saw another check ever. I was in charge of paying for the cats and bird food at this point, and so losing the money devastated me. I stopped working there because they refused to only let me pick up my checks because I was still a minor. Instead when my sister moved in, I started stealing some of my mom's money to pay for food for my pets.

After I quit, I heard of this wonderful game that is on the rise and many of you would recognize the name, RuneScape. I played it every day that I could, any time I was allowed to. I would even go to the library just to play. I wasn't the only one as most of the people on the computer were playing it too when I went in. We owned four computers at the time, one in the mini-mall, one in Mom's chapel, and two in the computer room. At the mall I would play it, and when my brother got off of my computer in the computer room, I would play on it. The other one in there was my stepdad's. To this day, I don't think he ever slept in the bed that my mom and him had. Shortly after I learned about membership, I tricked him. I got him to try it for just five hours by just pestering him so much, even when he was fucking me. So he agreed to five hours. A week later he got membership for himself, so I complained that he was growing those skills without me. He paid for RuneScape membership for me for five years. It was my escape from reality besides books, which no longer held my attention as much thanks to everything going on.

This place is where I learned that I like golf, and so my mom signed me up for golf club at the YMCA, as well as bowling. She was always outwardly proud of me for doing both of them besides my job, however at home she was pissed that I would only play RuneScape. I did get straight *A*s through my school life; however, school was easy for me. I wouldn't say I had a perfect memory, but I never studied for tests and still got *A*s or 100 percent if they used that grade system. Those were just my extra stuffs. At school I was in choir, band, art, and different clubs depending on what worked that season. I wasn't home that often thanks to all the extra activities I was in. When I was in eighth grade, Mom lost the mini-mall thanks to the owner of the buildings wanting it all back. She moved the wedding chapel to another place, however, which we stayed in for a year. I had to share my bedroom with his computer room at that time, so I left a lot more to other things.

I still took care of my pets, but I wasn't home much until Mom got me into my own little apartment. It was technically all three of ours. It was a studio, so I slept in the kitchen while she got the "bedroom" portion of it. Even though I was the one who was in there more, and she slept in the chapel more often than the apartment, I still had the kitchen only. That summer I went to my dad's house because Mom let me, and I thought it would be better to get away from my stepdad. My dad lived with his sister and his wife. The wife hated me from the start. Said I was a stuck-up bitch as I wouldn't talk to her, or do things she liked. By this time I was pretty independent as I was doing small jobs here and there through school so I could make enough to feed my small household. My dad got me an algebra textbook that summer as I was going into algebra in eighth grade. It was a privilege in my school for the top ten math students in seventh grade. I thought that home was wonderful. How wrong I learned I was later.

In eighth grade, Dad started sending me and my mom more money to help with my pursuits. Even told her to send receipts to show she was spending the money on me, and not herself. Apparently he threatened to take me away if she didn't use his money on me. So I got a set of golf clubs, I got art supplies, I would get clothes, even a small allowance. He even sent money to pay for my school lunches, though I only spent half of it, hiding the rest in books and other things trying to save. At the mini-mall, I met my first official boyfriend and I tried to get him to get me out before I was even thirteen. When I learned he was just as helpless as his parents were not super rich, I tried dropping him. He stalked me, though, through RuneScape, Yahoo, everything.

The only good time I remember besides finally having everything I needed in eighth grade is that I worked as a volunteer at the haunted house in the town. Each of the towns had a haunted house. The one in my town was for teens and adults with a lot scarier spots. The other town had a childcare type thing. You could take your kid there, let them check the kids candy for metal, and then the kid stayed until 9:00 p.m. They had a small haunted house too, but it was catered to young ones. In eighth grade I helped with the older one every day after school. I also volunteered at the library as my mom told me colleges liked kids who volunteered. I only got to try out Halloween when I got to seventh grade because Halloween is "devil's worship." I think I only came home for sleep most of the time, and to feed my pets. He couldn't touch me if I wasn't home, so I stayed away as much as possible.

The last place with my last stepdad. We moved when I was in ninth grade, same town, same landlord, but we finally got a bedroom! Here is when my stepdad took me to a sex shop and bought toys just to use on me. Here is where I also remember yelling at Mom that I wouldn't clean another dish ever again. I also picked up a job as a babysitter on Sunday's and, lady, if you ever read this you still owe me insane amounts of money. I was to be paid $5 an hour, I would only get $20 even though every Sunday I was there from 8:00 a.m.–10:00 p.m. I was babysitting a toddler and an infant, as well as cleaning her dishes and cooking for them. Anyways here I learned my cat, who was indoor and outdoor cat, had tricked the whole neighborhood to feed him or shelter him for me.

If I was struggling to pay for food that month, he would go ask neighbors for wet food, and when Mom locked him out of the house, he tricked a school classmate into letting him in for the night. Tiger was the neighborhood cat, not just mine. Cookie was given up after the mini-mall as his health was declining and my mom had a rich friend who would take him in and help him. Before ninth grade, I don't know about all of you, but we could chose even our main courses for high school. However I needed my parents' approval for any classes I picked out of the standard flow. So when I went to my mom to sign, she saw I took out ones she wanted me in, band and choir, choosing more computer classes. She erased my whole list, and put what she said would be better for a music major in college. I didn't want to go to college for music, I might play clarinet and sing, but anyone who hits a bad note I can hear and it makes me flinch. I couldn't put up with it anymore but she insisted. My life, even though college was planned out before I was even in ninth grade.

Ninth grade started and only the first half of ninth grade did I complete in her care. Now, keep in mind, I was still volunteering in the library, I was tutoring kids in school, as well as cooking cakes for Mom's wedding chapel. I was babysitting Sundays, while Saturdays was the household laundry at the Laundromat, and I wasn't eating at home as there wasn't much in there. I dove into anime at this point. It was my escape from my escape. My room wasn't just my room; it held the tuxes for the men, the bridesmaid dresses, and the veils. I never got privacy as Mom would pull strangers into my room without my say. Not even a knock on the door to announce it. She would just walk in with them even if I was dressing for school. I learned how to dress in my clothes under the covers. I was so hyperaware of everything that I fell asleep at about 2:30 or 3:00 a.m. every day.

I would need to wake at six, however, to shower and get to school by 7:30 since it took about thirty minutes to walk to school uphill. This is the house that I told my mom to stop showering me. I was still so afraid of water I couldn't even shower, but in this house I couldn't handle the red burns on my skin as she put the hot on high, and scrubbed me tell I was red all over. With the lack of sleep I had, I told her to stop and let me. I wasn't allowed to lock the bathroom door, though, so if my stepdad wanted to come in, he could. She could also let clients come in while I am there. I had to be aware of everything, every sound, every movement, every breath that was happening in the house at all times.

I wasn't mentally doing well at all, and right after Halloween I tried to take my life. It didn't work, as the knife I used was dull, after the first cut my bird started screaming at me. I looked at him with tears and realized that if I die no one would feed him. I was pulling my babies into the grave with me and I couldn't do that to them. I stopped for that week.

I told my mom I needed help in therapy when I tried a second time, to which she took me to one. This woman, though, should have been removed from there. She had told me that everything was my fault. I was too sexy for my stepdad. I was too dumb for my mom to see me otherwise, many other things. She even said that my brother's mental issues and my sister's kids were my fault. The last time I went there, she tried to get me to believe that people being trans and gay is also my fault.

I walked out of her session and told Mom I am fine and don't need to come back. Two days later on my third attempt I called my dad and begged him to take me away. I was only fourteen at the time, almost fifteen. He dropped everything, told his boss what was going on, and was given PTO to come grab me. I told my mom the next day and for the next three days she showered me with food, with gifts, with anything she thought would keep me there. When he still showed up, she tried to send him home, but he had flung open the door and got me, my bird and my cat out of there. My dad at the time was my savior, but man I was wrong about him.

Before I get into the rest of it, I want to talk a bit about other things that happened to me that I don't know when it happened clearly, but I remember them happening. Mom owned a restaurant that I was taking plates to, even though I could hardly lift the plates. When someone important parked, Mom would send me to my corner and I was allowed to play with my five toys which included a puzzle. One day a judge came in, saw me sitting alone, and joined me. She told Mom that I have an artist's eye, but I seem analytical, and might do well in a law field. At some point I was sent to a Christian camp, and while I don't have trauma there, I did learn that I have a smoke issue. I can't be around a campfire without my lungs burning almost immediately, this is important for later.

At some point before age two, I was put in a shopping basket backwards which messed my ankles up so bad that when they got home they couldn't move my feet or ankles without me screaming for over an hour. We never got that checked out and I twist my ankle a lot, even now. I can't drink milk, but my mom would always have cereal and milk in the house, telling me I am allowed to eat that in the house without issues. I also was only allowed to use the bathroom for one hour a week until I left, and that includes shower times. My brother introduced me to *The Mummy* when I was little, and I had to be told by a doctor that movies are not real. Even now nothing scares me anymore as I have seen real demons in human flesh. After my first period, my mom posted on Facebook she is now "selling" her kid to the highest bidder as she is a woman now. I know the Grim Reaper. I have almost died enough times through my life that we are on good terms for now.

DAD

I moved to live with my dad right before my fifteenth. He was still with his sister and wife. I got the third and smallest bedroom at that time when I moved in, but I didn't care because I was away from them. Dixie and Tiger were still with me, and I thought it was going to be good. We did move to two other houses besides this one, one to let me have more space in my place and the last one after my dad left my stepmom. I finally made one super strong friend, who is still a friend to this day. She saw me after we moved. We didn't live in that original home for long and moved within two months. We clicked so fast, every weekend we would spend it at the other's house. I had food for days in that house, and I was encouraged to learn how to cook. I learned magic, and I learned how toxic my "boyfriend" from RuneScape was. My friend stayed with me for that first school year when her family moved, but she needed to finish that school year. We opened our doors to her, and she left after that year. That first year was so enjoyable mostly. I did only sleep about four hours a day except on Thursday's when I came home from school and would pass out, not waking to anything until 6:00 a.m. Nothing could wake me, and this kept going for years. Thursdays I wouldn't wake at all. She was with me even when I woke up one day and started ripping up my old stuff. My best friend is my everything. Sorry had to get that out first before I dive into more issues.

Those Thursdays were really bad for me, I would come home so tired I was dragging myself just to get to bed. My sweet sixteenth was a Friday, so I planned to just sleep Thursday and welcome Friday with more energy. When I opened my eyes at 4:00 a.m., my dad had tied me down and gagged me. He was currently raping me. My savior was doing the thing I ran from, on my birthday even. Once he was done he released me and before he left he told me that as his flesh and blood, he can do whatever he wants. Every week after that I woke up on Fridays with him inside or trying to get inside me. I just gave up at this point. I knew it would only last until I moved out, however, and so I counted those days when I turned eighteen and had money of my own. He never did anything else bad to me except he would force me to have sex with him every week or masturbate in front of me. I just kept going to school and kept going. At the last house, we had in this state, he got me a dog, Princess. She was my world, and she almost bit his dick off the first time he came and did that to me again. I slept with her every night, knowing I was protected. She was only a small dog, but she was willing to fight him for me. The last house we stayed in until he lost his job thanks to the housing market crash.

The amount of good memories I had after I had Princess increased so much that I could spend pages, just talking about her. I'll keep bringing her up here and there, but she was just like Tiger and Dixie, my child. We had to move to some Southern states to get him a new job, and we planned to take Tiger, Dixie, and Princess with us. However, they tricked me to taking Tiger outside of the trailer to get in the car when my uncle's dog chased him. The breakaway collar came off and he ran. I never saw Tiger again as my aunt and dad refused to look for him and just drove away without him. So we only had Princess and Dixie for two years.

The first year I quit school and took my GED because in all three moves I lost all my school credits and was still in ninth grade. I was going to be seventeen, even though this school said they would transfer my credits after I was in the school for that last half year for ninth grade, they told me I would have to take the first part. I was done, I quit, and a few months later got my GED instead. I had only finished half of ninth grade in each move so apparently I lost all my credits and I was tired of going into ninth grade when I was tutoring classmates all the time. I also saw getting my GED as a step in finding a job. I wanted to run as soon as I could.

The second year my aunt decided to move back to the first state because their sister needed help. She moved away from us and my dad and I moved into a military retire-type home. My father was military, so he did qualify for it at least for one year while I was still technically not an adult. I had found out that my stalker from RuneScape lived in this state the first year, and had visited him several times. I couldn't take it anymore there and after I got a job, I told him that he either has to step up and help me find a home for him and myself or we are done. He moved up to us, and then got a job where I worked. He lost it after a month due to pretending to be sick at work so he didn't have to work. I quit working there months later because I got promoted to Team Lead without the training, without the pay but all the responsibilities. I even would get chewed out if I didn't do something that was part of my job title. I couldn't handle that kind of toxic work environment. I took my dad's job, though, when his health was failing and he moved back with his sister.

My stalker was already working at that job before me, but when I started it got worse. I would have to work his shift as well as mine because I couldn't drive. I would have to go in with him late at night and then in the morning work my shift. Or if I had the afternoon, I would work that, then be stuck there until the morning shift. If I didn't help him do his job, then I got chewed out as the owner was sexist and believed women served men. I also had to tie his shoes as he didn't know how. He didn't know how to cross the street. He didn't even shower before he met me. He didn't know how to be human, let alone an adult. But I had "known" him for years and he was willing to help me get out of my house from my dad. Princess was still with us, but Dixie was given up to my cousin when the landlord said that we were allowed one pet, not two and birds count. So my cousin, who couldn't have kids and was allergic to fur got to take care of my bird. Dixie however turned out was in stage four lung cancer.

When I had him, he showed no signs, even my cousin said that when I came over he seemed healthy. When I left, he would collapse being unable to do anything. Before the month was out, he passed and my cousin convinced my dad to just not let me over to her house until she could tell me. She didn't tell me for over a year. At that time I couldn't do or say anything, I had Princess and a man child to take care of.

I lived with my stalker for two and a half years. Half a year was with my dad, then a year in a small apartment that we were sleeping on the floor, and I was not there mentally. I was doing all the chores of the house and working both of our shifts. The owner said he would still get a paycheck if he was at work, but if he wasn't there, I would get the money so he was there a lot. The second year, we did move closer, and I brought my best friend down to us. She helped me get the strength to leave him finally, even though that meant financially we were worse off. I called the only one who I knew would help, my dad. He came and got me and her from that situation. We moved in with him and my aunt. We shared a bedroom, a bathroom and later a job in that state. We had a fight and to this day I still feel bad about it. Her mom got her out of our house after the fight but living 24/7 with someone is really stressful. Don't worry Princess was still in my life then, so my dad was a lot tamer for a bit.

We kept bouncing from house to house for a while, while I worked one or two jobs at a time to support their spending habits. I saw none of my own money the years before I kicked them out. My dad and aunt were actually on disability and retirement money, making over $2500 per month together, and the most expensive apartment we had was only $800. However, I had to have a job as they couldn't afford my insurance, or anything else I wanted. I needed to have my own money still coming in but out of each month, I think I saw maybe $200. I couldn't leave either as Princess held me to a house. I needed to keep her safe. I didn't care what happened to me. She couldn't be stuck outside with me. I put up with it until my aunt couldn't take him anymore and moved out, I learned later he was forcing himself on her too.

My brother died sometime during this time and while I wasn't that sad about it, I still tried to get PTO for his funeral and my job wouldn't even give me the days off. It was really bad for sick days too. So when she left, he started going after me more even with Princess protecting me. Finally I threw him out as I couldn't take it anymore. I knew financially I could handle the house on my own. I knew I had a well-paying job, I could drive, I had a car, and I could do it. Then I learned my dad was taking my checks still from my bank account. I only got $50 a check to survive on, and my apartment was $600. I couldn't keep it, but I did try to keep it as best I could for a year. At this point I met the girls.

SISTER

I'm going to keep the girls super brief as that is our story and not just mine. They let me live in their new apartment after I sheltered them using my own apartment. Later on they admitted feelings for me, and I helped keep that going because I didn't understand love. We became homeless and living in a car in a new state after that year there trying to make it. We were in a car until about May. At that point they broke my heart and told me to get out of the car. I called my best friend's cousin as well as my sister. I refused to talk to my mom still and my dad had passed while we were homeless, so I was just trying to figure out what to do. My sister came to get me in that state, three states over. But first she tried to tell the women's protection services in that state that my exes were human traffickers. She just wanted to use state funds to come pick me up, but that isn't right either.

I didn't learn about that until after I was back in the starting state that we left and that my dad died in. At this point I had Harley, Quinn, and Princess. Harley and Quinn were cats, and when my sister came to get me, she was upset that my cats didn't like being in a cage. She said they should be happy we are taking them at all. When we got to the old state, she said I was allowed to look through my stuff in the storage unit and get what I wanted and needed and she would be back in a hour to get me so we could get a hotel room with her two kids. I agreed as it seemed fine, she left me Princess and took Harley and Quinn. An hour passed and I told my sister I sorted what I wanted and was ready for her. Two hours passed, nothing from her. Four hours later she calls me and says that she gave Harley and Quinn to the shelter. I had twelve hours to decide if I wanted to keep Princess and stay homeless here, or give her up and take myself into the hospital. I had told her how unstable I was without my pets because they were my world, and she decided to take my support away. I had no choice. I tried calling my exes to get my aunt's number, and they told me what she did there and that I wasn't allowed to contact them again. I was stuck in a storage unit for twelve hours to decide. I called the cops, and gave up Princess. It's been almost three years and I am still upset about that. I went to the hospital and told them how bad I was, and they put me in a ward.

The next day I called my sister telling her just to leave without me as I will figure out how to take care of myself here. She didn't, even blaming me for going into the hospital, telling me she just wanted something to put me to sleep so she could put me in her state's ward. I told her to fuck off and leave me alone. Then I called them about Princess and gave up my claim completely. I was in there for two or three weeks, made friends, and was released with another girl. She let me stay at her place for a few days, I even set us up with food bank items as I didn't have a job. She came home after that day and kicked me out as she found out my exes were being prosecuted as human traffickers and she didn't want criminals in her house. She wouldn't even listen to my side of the story and just kicked me out.

I ended back in the ward as I lost everything again due to my sister. After being in there again for a while, I got out, and called my best friend's cousin again. He told me to let my sister back in because she seems to really care about me. I did, I don't regret it, but at the time I really did. She came one more time to pick me up, this time when she took me over, she took me to the one place I told her I wouldn't be able to live in—Mom's house. My stepdad had already died years ago, but I couldn't forget what my mom put me through, the mental strain, the physical abuse, I couldn't handle her. My mom pretty much dragged me out of my sister's car. My sister then proceeded to take all my belongings, and my phone and told me when SHE says I am healthy, I will have my items back. I lost all my items, my computer, my phone, my clothes, my books, and everything that reminded me of Princess. Everything.

Now let's forget me for a minute and talk about my sister before I left Mom to set the stage properly. In 2000 she had her first child, and she wasn't eighteen yet, so she was forced to give the kid up. She had no choice to keep her and it turns out that my first niece is blind, but I know that not from her birth, you'll see why soon. Her second kid, my first nephew was when we owned the mini-mall. She hyped my mom up letting her know she would be a proper grandma for this kid. She had already adopted him out before birth however, and after the parents got him, they changed his name so he would never know his mom. Her third child, was born out of an abusive relationship she was in. The fourth was also from him, but he didn't know about him at all.

Before the fourth was a year old, they both were taken from her as there were signs of physical abuse on both kids. I was already gone by then, but if anyone had asked me I would have told them how I saw her throw her youngest at a wall for touching her computer. She had five and six when I called her. They were the oldest kids she had ever had, being nine and six. She was still abusing them, but she knew how to be subtle about it now. The abuse that happened in that house is my niece's story, and hopefully my nephew doesn't even remember his mom. I will not approach that subject, but after moving to Mom's, I learned my sister had tracked down three of her other kids. She had plans to show up at her first child's house and bring her home because "I gave birth to her, so she is my property." My mom and grandmother have the same mindset, so did my dad honestly. So I know things about kid one, three, and four that I shouldn't know, and I did feel scared for them until this part. Here is how I made my sister go to jail.

I have avoided states I don't want people to easily link me to this story, but I have to point out where this all started with my sister. My sister, she took her boyfriend and her kids to California for a trip, picking up his mom and brother on the way. The night they arrived, him and her got into a fight because his mom refused to pay her extra for driving them to California with her. She called the cops saying he is physically abusive and they arrived at her hotel to see what happened. She was taken to jail instead, being more prone to violence than he was. Her kids, because her family was several states away, were put into a group home temporarily. Temporarily. She got out the next morning as she had calmed down, and when she got back to the hotel finds out that the kids are in a group home, and calls social services. As it was Saturday, they couldn't push the paperwork though to get them out early, but the lady said she can try to get them out on Tuesday into her custody instead of Thursday since she is out of jail.

An hour later my sister called my mom and said she was going to the group home and getting her kids back. When prodded she said she didn't have permission and she's not sure where they are, but she has an idea and if she sees her kids she will take them from the home. Mom tried to convince her that waiting until Tuesday would be the better option. Instead my sister sat outside the home, which I called and told them my sister's plans. They got the group home's security out there to get rid of her, and Sunday the lady told her the kids will remain in the home until Thursday. She had to come in Monday to convince them to let the kids come back.

Turns out that Sunday the kids were sent to a foster home to protect them, and she found out. No one asked and we told them not to let them have their watches, but they still put them on this whole time. There is a GPS in there my sister was able to track no matter where they were. She showed up to the porch of the foster home Sunday demanding to have her kids back. She came back Monday begging to see her kids. She had to be escorted off by the cops, and when she went to social services of California she demanded her kids back now as she can't afford to stay in California anymore. They told her that she can go home if she wants, and on Thursday, if their investigation proves nothing wrong in the house, they will be sent home. She stayed on the beach day one, day two she was with some sugar daddy. She lost the kids before Wednesday popped up by showing up daily to the foster mom's home, the youngest kid showing signs of drug withdrawal and other things. I don't know the full details and I don't want to know. She eventually was even told by her sugar daddy's lawyers that her home state's courts might be able to help more. She left California and went home.

The next week she calls my mom and tells her that she found her kids 120 miles from her home, and plans to kidnap them. She called the school they are in and asked to know if they are there. The kids were taken to school in a cop car for weeks thanks to that. They were not allowed outside except for school. She showed up to the house, on one of her visits she told her daughter how to run away from the home. She tried everything. Finally they decided she couldn't keep this up and finally sent them to daycare. My sister saw them outside, grabbed them both and fled. Mom, her best friend, myself, all the people she has wronged in her city, we all worked together to stop her. She got caught and sent to jail. Mom went to all her court hearings and one of them she literally showed how out of touch she was.

She told the judge that if he let her go in the next week, she can get a place and get her kids back within that week. She was put in for a few years, by the time she gets out the kids will be old enough to tell her to leave them alone. But she won't stop, they are her blood and so she believes they are her property. During all this, we lost all her storage units, including the one that my stuff was in, so I didn't get anything back ever. My sister is gone for years, but when she gets out if no one helped her in there, I will see to it that she is in a ward before she gets a foot near me or the kids again.

MOM, PART 2

So back to living with Mom, I lived in a different house than any of the others, even in a different town but the same state that my stepdad had been in. I was reminded everyday how bad it was as a kid. She never believed my sun allergy. She also didn't think I was mentally unstable because I was her perfect child no matter what. After moving back is when I remember that she had destroyed my body image but tell me as a kid I was fat and ugly. It all came rushing back when I saw my self-portrait my art teacher had me try to finish. I did finish it, but as soon as she pointed it out she told me how ugly I will always be. She also reminded me I don't have talent and could never amount to anything. I was in therapy still in her home, even was still on meds. Turns out the meds were messing with me more as I wasn't chemically imbalanced, I was traumatized. So I stopped the meds, stopped the therapy, got started in college, and got a cat, Buddy. I got stable quickly just with Buddy there, and even though I dropped out of college, I met the true love of my life. I also got a new job in another state just forty minutes away from my mom's. I want to completely leave her and all my past behind, however this job is too good to pass up.

DISABILITY

Now this part isn't fully trauma, but I want to point out that at my mom's, I tried to get disability. Most people who went through all of this, are not as stable as I am. I found out thanks to tests, and TikTok, I have ADHD, Autism, PTSD, Anxiety, and Depression. I also know that I can't feel hunger, or cold properly. I still have issues in the sun, and in heat. I pass out in 75+ weather in thirty minutes. I don't have proper circulation in my feet and they get cold if I do anything but lay down. My skull isn't fully attached anymore, and has to be moved back on every month. I have several spinal disks that are a lot thinner than they should be. I can't drink straight water without my body rejecting it thanks to copper poisoning as a kid.

My joints, I don't know if they come out all the way, but they do pop out a lot. My ankles get twisted daily. I'm in pain from wake to sleep no matter what I do, and it's at level-six pain all day. I have high blood pressure, which is now taken care of by medication. Its only six because I am taking fish oil, and Tylenol daily to help dull the pain. The days I forget to take my meds until super late, my pain is almost seven to eight easily. But I am so used to it, my pain scale is warped from normal scales. I have been to therapists, and even specialist doctors to see if anyone can put a concrete diagnosis on me so I can get on disability. No one says I am that disabled because I can ignore the pain. I can ignore the torture. I can ignore the PTSD. I am not disabled.

So knowing my past, knowing my story, knowing my physical health, am I disabled? Cause I think I am fine for now. I will live my life knowing that my home failed me, the children protective services failed me, and the government failed me. I want someone out there to know my story, though, and know that you may be in hell but even if everything is failing you something, or someone will be there for you. There is something out there that will support you, even if the systems in place fail.

Jessica Bourquin

Thank you for reading this far.
I hope it reaches at least one person.

Written by Jessica.
Helped by Buddy.

Keep fighting, something is out there for you.